DATE DUE

HIGHSMITH 45-227

Sports Stars

TONY DORSETT

From Heisman to Super Bowl in One Year

By Dick Conrad

CHILDRENS PRESS, CHICAGO

Cover photograph: United Press International Photo
Inside photographs courtesy of the following: Bill Smith, pages 6, 8, 16, 36, 38, 39, 40, and 43; United Press International, pages 10, 14, 31, 32, and 34; and George Gojkovich, pages 18, 20, 21, 23, 26, and 28.

Library of Congress Cataloging in Publication Data

Conrad, Dick.
   Tony Dorsett, from Heisman to Super Bowl in one year.

   (Sports stars)
   SUMMARY: A biography of the Heisman Trophy winner who was named the 1977 NFL Rookie of the Year.
   1. Dorsett, Tony—Juvenile literature. 2. Football players—United States—Biography. [1. Dorsett, Tony. 2. Football players. 3. Afro-Americans—Biography] I. Title. II. Series.
GV939.D67C66   796.33'2'0924 [B] [92]   78-11378
ISBN 0-516-04305-6

New 1982 Edition.

Copyright© 1979 by Regensteiner Publishing Enterprises, Inc.
All rights reserved. Published simultaneously in Canada.
Printed in the United States of America.

9 10 11 12 R 85 84 83 82

Sports Stars

TONY DORSETT

From Heisman to Super Bowl in One Year

Dallas Cowboy Tony Dorsett wears the number 33.

It was a hot, sticky August afternoon. Soon the 1977 football season would start. The Dallas Cowboys were practicing. The players were not supposed to tackle hard. But one player had just been injured.

Coach Tom Landry spoke through a megaphone. He called out, "Dorsett, get in the backfield."

Tony Dorsett was a high-priced rookie running back. He had hurt his knee that week and had not practiced much.

Quarterback Roger Staubach barked out signals. The ball was snapped. Staubach handed it off to Dorsett. Dorsett dodged two tacklers. He ran around the line. Practice or not, safety Cliff

Dorsett jokes with teammate Tony Hill.

Harris did not want anyone to get around him. He dove for the fast Dorsett. He grabbed his foot. Dorsett flew into the air. He slid to a stop on the sidelines. Then he sat up. He clutched his knee. He had a look of pain on his face. He mumbled, "My knee. My knee."

For an instant the field was silent. The players stopped and stared. Suddenly, Tony Dorsett sprang to his feet. He grinned. "Just jivin'," he said. "Just jivin'."

Some players laughed. But not coach Landry. He glared at Dorsett. Landry said nothing. But his icy look meant only one thing: "Dorsett, don't you ever do that again."

Tony makes an eight-yard gain during a Dallas Cowboy-Baltimore Colt exhibition game in August, 1977.

Tony needed this little joke. He was under great pressure at the Cowboy training camp.

Since his first day there, reporters had bothered him. They wanted interviews. Photographers wanted his picture. News people stayed close to him. If he even sneezed, it was in the papers.

"I think the reason so many people are interested in me is because they realize the spot I'm in with the Cowboys. They've built me up as the guy who's going to change the Dallas Cowboys. I'm the new look for them. The scatback."

Tony was something new for Dallas. The Cowboys had never had a runner like Gale Sayers, O.J. Simpson, or Walter Payton. That kind of back can get very fast touchdowns. The Dallas fans hoped Tony would be a great halfback.

The reporters didn't give Tony much peace. But he was always polite to them. "I enjoy talking to the press," he said. "It makes me feel good." He liked to be doing something important. Important enough for people to want to talk to him about it.

He had not always been such an open person. As a child, he had been very shy. The shyness started early.

He grew up in Aliquippa, Pennsylvania. Aliquippa is a small, steel-mill town near Pittsburgh. His neighborhood was not a slum. But it was a tough, working-class area. Being good in sports was the best way to earn respect there.

Tony was a small, thin child. He was afraid to face bigger boys on the football field. He was good at avoiding contact. So good that he hardly ever got his pants dirty. After the games, on his way home, he would roll on the ground. His pants would pick up some dirt and grass stains. Then he could tell big stories about the rough games he had played. He felt he had to keep up with his brothers.

Tony's older brothers were good in sports. They were neighborhood stars.

"My brothers were good athletes," Tony says. "While I was growing up, people told me I was the worst. The sorriest of the Dorsett brothers." They said Tony wouldn't amount to anything.

Dorsett on the way to a touchdown against the Chicago Bears in December, 1977, during his first season with the Dallas Cowboys.

When Tony entered high school he was still small. But he played better football. He had the gift of speed. He could run faster than everyone in the neighborhood. When he started running down a football field, the others gave up. They didn't even try to chase him.

Tony became a good high-school football player. But he didn't grow much. He wondered if he could be a good college player.

During his junior year in high school something happened to Tony. He would never forget it. He had driven to the steel mill to pick up his father from work. This was the first time he had been allowed to do this. As he waited in the parking lot, he saw a man. He was covered with grime.

Dorsett getting away from the defense during a Dallas-St. Louis game.

The man's face had a look of great tiredness. He walked very slowly. He walked toward Tony's car. The man opened the door of the car. He got inside. He started talking. It was only then that Tony realized that the man was his father. He hadn't even recognized him.

"My dad always told me not to get stuck in the steel mills. And that day convinced me," Tony said years later. "I made up my mind right then that I'd be a great football player."

Tony Dorsett became the best high-school halfback in the state of Pennsylvania. As his graduation day drew near, college coaches came to his door. One coach made the best impression on Tony. That was Johnny Majors.

Tony Dorsett wore the same number—33—during his college years with the University of Pittsburgh that he wears now as a Cowboy.

Majors had once been a star running back at the University of Tennessee. He had just become the new coach at the University of Pittsburgh. Pitt had a losing record. Tony liked the idea of helping the team become a winner.

When he started at Pitt Tony was only 5 feet, 10 inches tall. He weighed less than 160 pounds. Most of the men on his offensive line were young. They were only first- or second-year players. Just as Tony was. But in his freshman year, Tony played hard. He wriggled, squirmed, and dodged. He gained more than 1,500 yards. This was amazing for a freshman.

Tony was very shy in his first season. But he began to come out of his shell. "My success in

In the Pitt games shown in these pictures, Tony had already developed a very smooth running style.

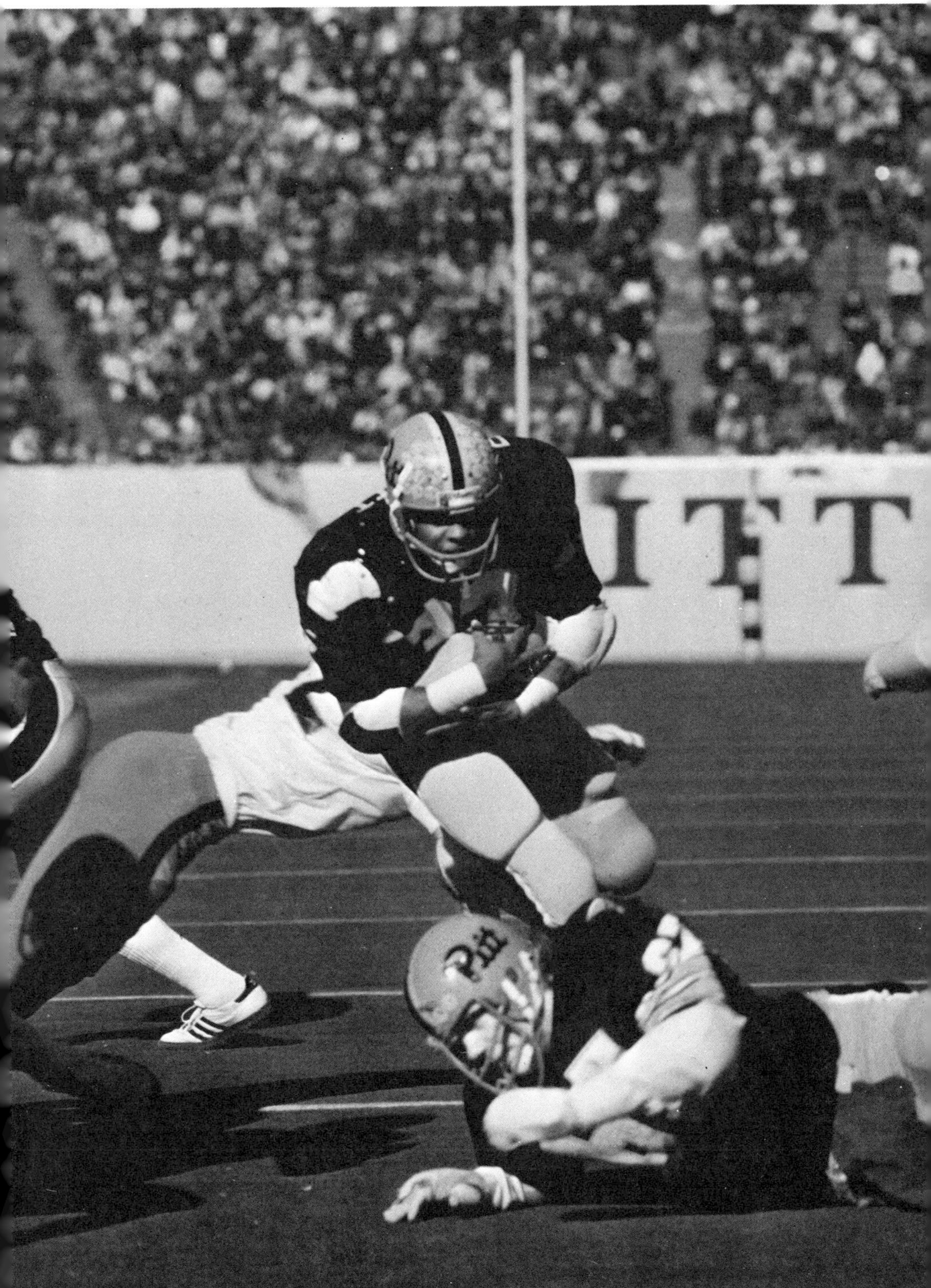
ITT
Pitt

football helped me a lot," he said. "I figured, hey, I'm a good player. Why should I be afraid to talk to a newspaperman? Or go on TV?"

On TV, fans saw a handsome man. He looks a lot like a young Flip Wilson. Tony began to like publicity. He went out of his way to promote the Pitt Panthers. He once wore a Superman costume for a magazine picture.

At Pitt, Dorsett began to show a certain running style. A very smooth style. When Dorsett runs down the field, he doesn't seem to be running. He seems to be gliding.

Coach Johnny Majors has seen many running backs. Tony, he says is one of the great ones.

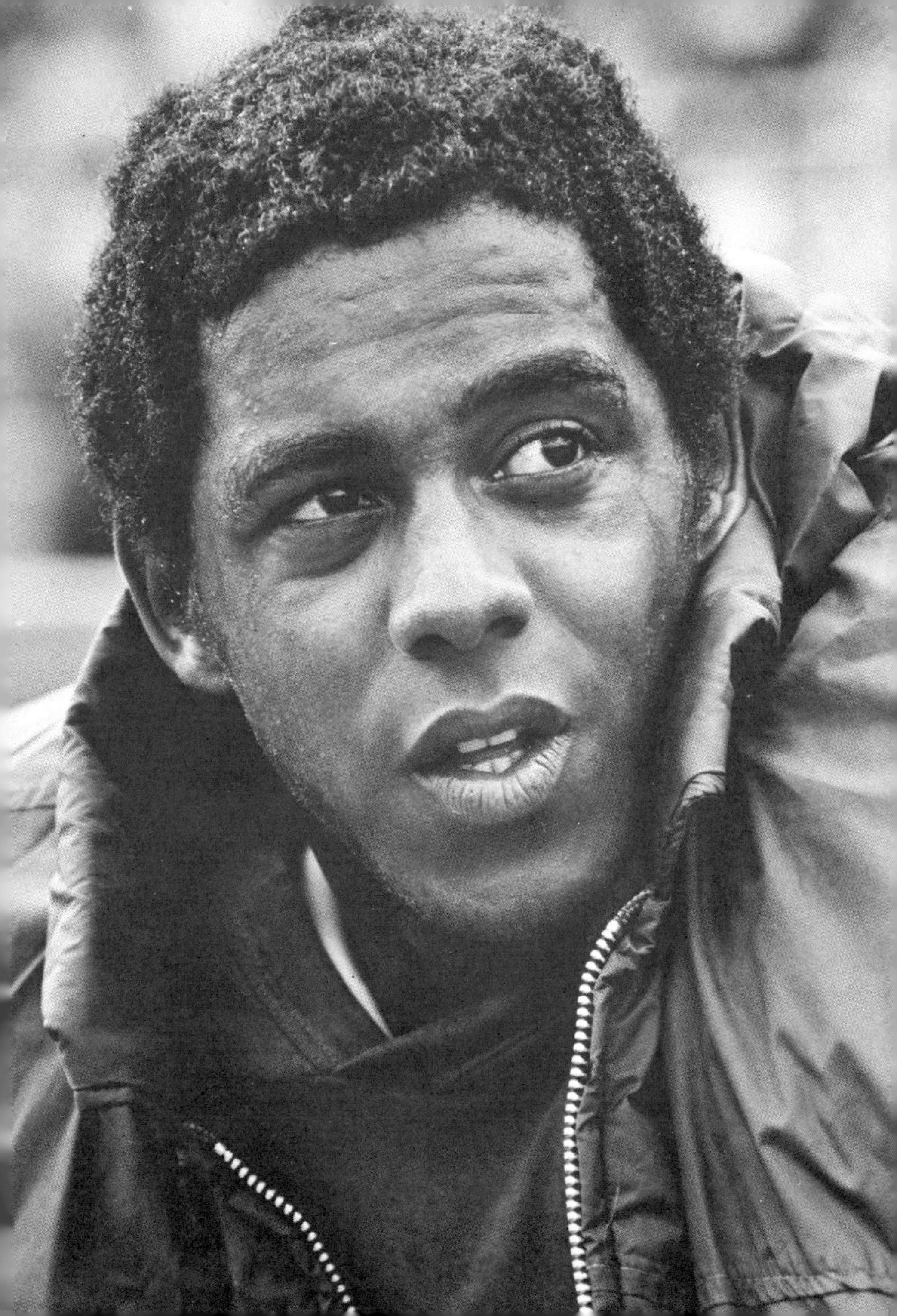

"We just flip him the ball and let him take off. I've never seen a back with his speed. And when you have that much speed, it's tough to cut and change directions. But Tony can. He can stop dead on a dime, take three little bitty steps, and be off again."

Majors also says Tony "has the heart to back up his feet. He won't shrink from a challenge. When one presents itself he gets tougher."

Tony had a great senior year. He had the best season of any running back in college football history.

The first game was against Notre Dame. Majors said later, "On our first play Notre Dame had us pinned deep in our own territory. We called a direct dive up the middle. Tony squirmed through a hole, broke three tackles, slipped, and slid. He nearly took my breath away. He ran for 61 yards. And it broke Notre Dame's heart."

The win against Notre Dame was the beginning. It got the University of Pittsburgh off to a great start. The Panthers became a super power.

In a game against Navy, Dorsett ran wild. He gained 180 yards. At the end of the game, his career rushing total was 5,206 yards. Twenty-nine yards more than the former record. That record had been set by Archie Griffin of Ohio State a year before. Tony had rushed for more yards than any other college running back.

Here Tony is shown as he gains some of the 303 yards he gained in the 1975 game against Notre Dame. In Pittsburgh's first game of the 1976 season, Tony's senior year, he gained 61 yards against Notre Dame. Pitt won the game and went on to an unbeaten season. Tony himself left college with a rushing record of 6,082 yards.

Breaking the old record was not enough for Tony. He wanted to set a record that would never be beaten. He wanted to gain more than 6,000 yards.

"Impossible," said a reporter. "You have only four games left this season. To get 6,000 you'd have to average almost 200 yards a game. Not even you can do that."

Tony just shrugged. "We'll see."

In the last game of the season the Pitt Panthers played Penn State. On the first play of the second half Dorsett charged up the middle. He gained 7 yards. Then he swept around the end for 3. Then, bingo! Dorsett streaked up the middle for 40 yards. And a touchdown. The rest of the game went the same way.

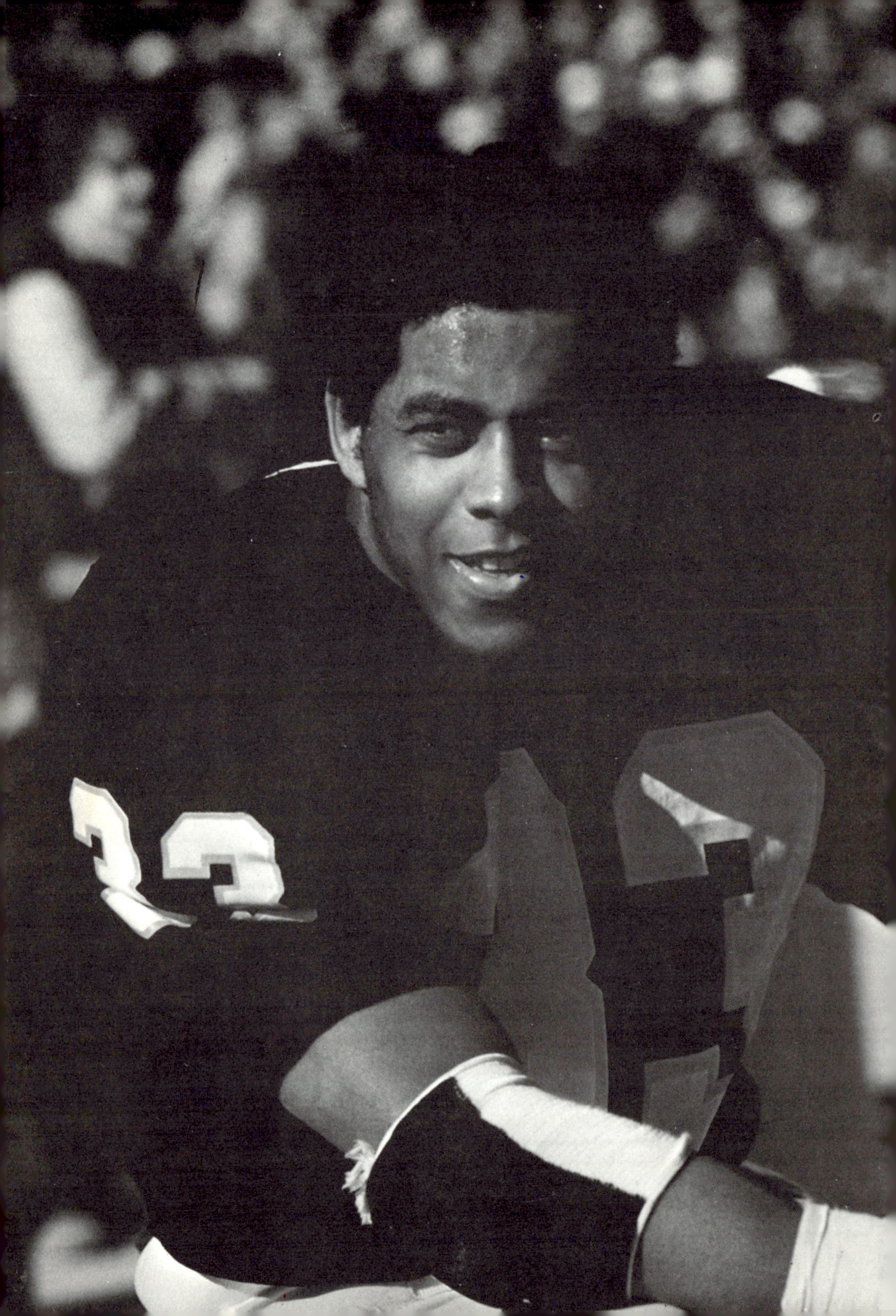

The University of Pittsburgh had had an unbeaten season. They capped it off by thrashing Penn State 24 to 7. Tony gained 224 yards. This put him above the 6,000-yard mark. He left college with a rushing record of 6,082 yards.

Tony said, "I'll take pride in every record I set. I wanted to be Number One. And I want to be that for as long as I live."

He probably will be. His 6,082-yard record will be very hard to beat.

Tony is a team player. He said of his Pitt Panthers, "All we've accomplished won't mean anything if we don't win the national championship." Standing between Pitt and the championship were the Georgia Bulldogs. They would meet in the

Sugar Bowl. On New Year's Day, Pitt beat Georgia 27 to 3. They completed a perfect 12-0 season. The Pitt Panthers were now the number one team in the nation.

Tony Dorsett was given the Heisman Trophy for 1976. This is a great honor for a college player. Tony had wanted it for a long time.

"The Heisman was a goal I set for myself when I was a freshman," he said. "I wanted to win it for Pitt, Coach Majors, myself, and my parents." Winning the Heisman meant a lot to Tony. It meant he was the best college football player in the United States.

In 1977, Tony went to Dallas. He got a five-year, million-dollar contract. He bought his par-

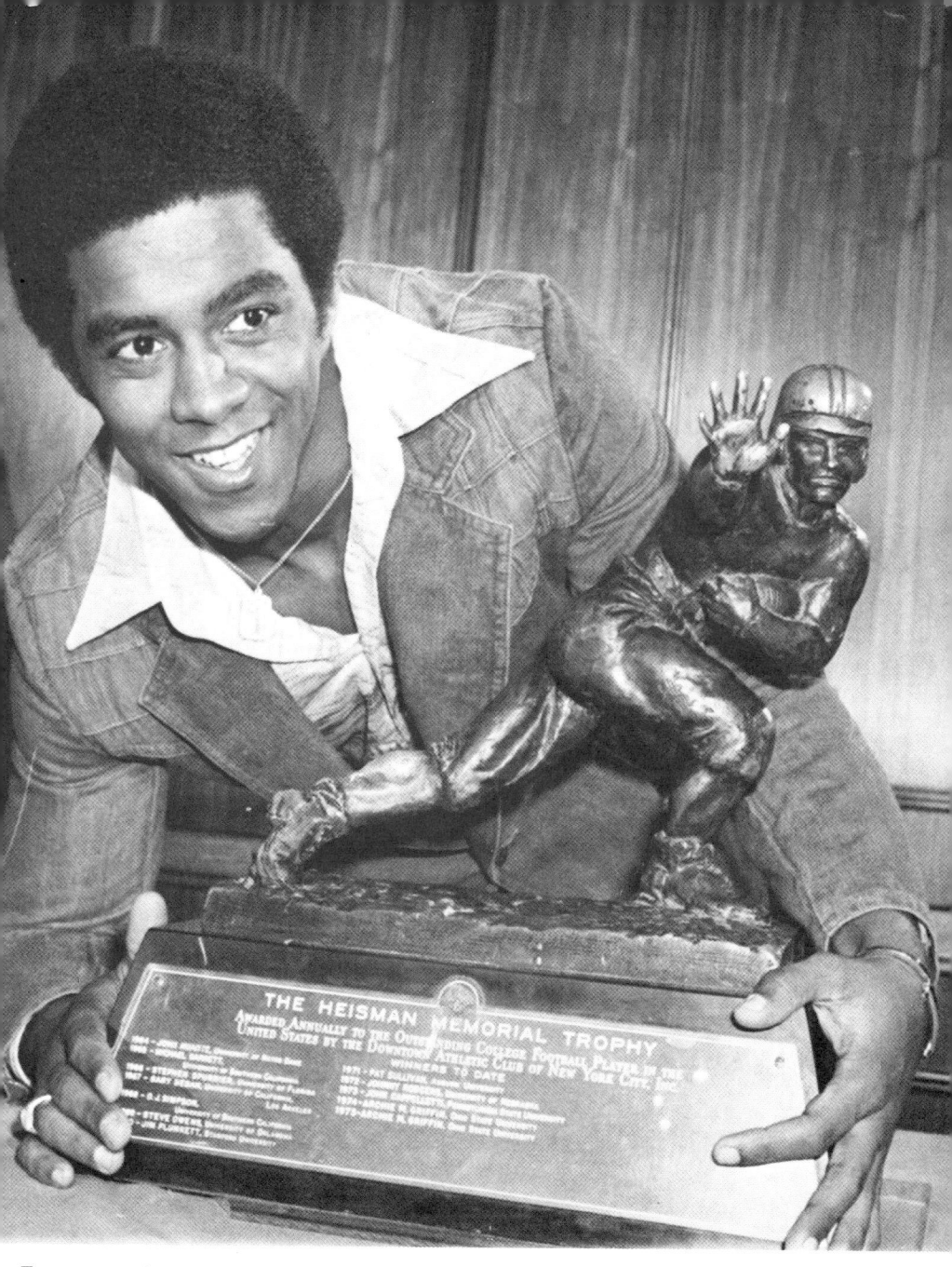

Tony smiles behind the Heisman Trophy, awarded to him in 1976.

A happy Tony Dorsett signed the contract with the Dallas Cowboys on May 26, 1977 (above). Here he is shown with (left to right) Harvey Eger, his attorney; Mike Troupe, his agent; and Gil Brandt, Dallas Cowboy vice president.

ents a new house in Aliquippa. He made another change. From then on he wanted his name pronounced Dor**sett**. He wanted the accent on the last syllable.

"The name is French," Tony said. "I liked the sound of it." He wanted to see what would happen on TV. He introduced himself as Tony Dor**sett**. Just to see what kind of reaction he'd get.

Just what was the reaction?

"It was negative. Just as I thought," Tony said. " 'Wow, what's he trying to do?' 'He's big-headed.' 'He thinks he's too much.' " That's what people said.

How he said his name made little difference. Most of his Dallas teammates would call him TD.

Shortly after he was drafted by the Cowboys, Tony shows off his new Cowboy jersey with the number 33.

These are his initials. It is also the short way to say "touchdown." So, in Dallas, the Cowboys waited for the arrival of TD.

The Dallas coaches were impressed by his speed. "I saw his ability when he was running on the first day," said Dan Reeves, assistant coach. "He was getting open without using fakes. He was just a blur against the linebackers. I had never seen anyone turn it on like that. I've never been on a team with or coached a back with Dorsett's speed. 4.45 for the 40. That's flying."

In the Cowboy's home opener against the New York Giants, Tony took a handoff and cut right. It was supposed to be a routine play. He found the hole sealed up and cut back left. He was looking

In a game against St. Louis, Cowboy Tony Dorsett evades a member of the St. Louis defense and keeps on running.

for running room. He gained a few yards. Then the defense cut him off again. So Tony retraced his steps. He darted right again. He slipped, squirmed, and broke a tackle. Finally, he dove into the end zone. He had made a great 34-yard touchdown run.

Walter Payton of the Chicago Bears watched a Dallas game on TV. He said Dorsett is "like a pinball runner, making cuts and unbelievable moves. He is starting a new era with the Cowboys."

Tony changed the Dallas game. His presence helped the Cowboys' passing. "When Tony comes in," said receiver Drew Pearson, "the secondary moves up closer. That gives me a better chance to get behind them."

Tony signs autographs after a game in Dallas. The picture on the opposite page shows his car with the initials T.D. on the door.

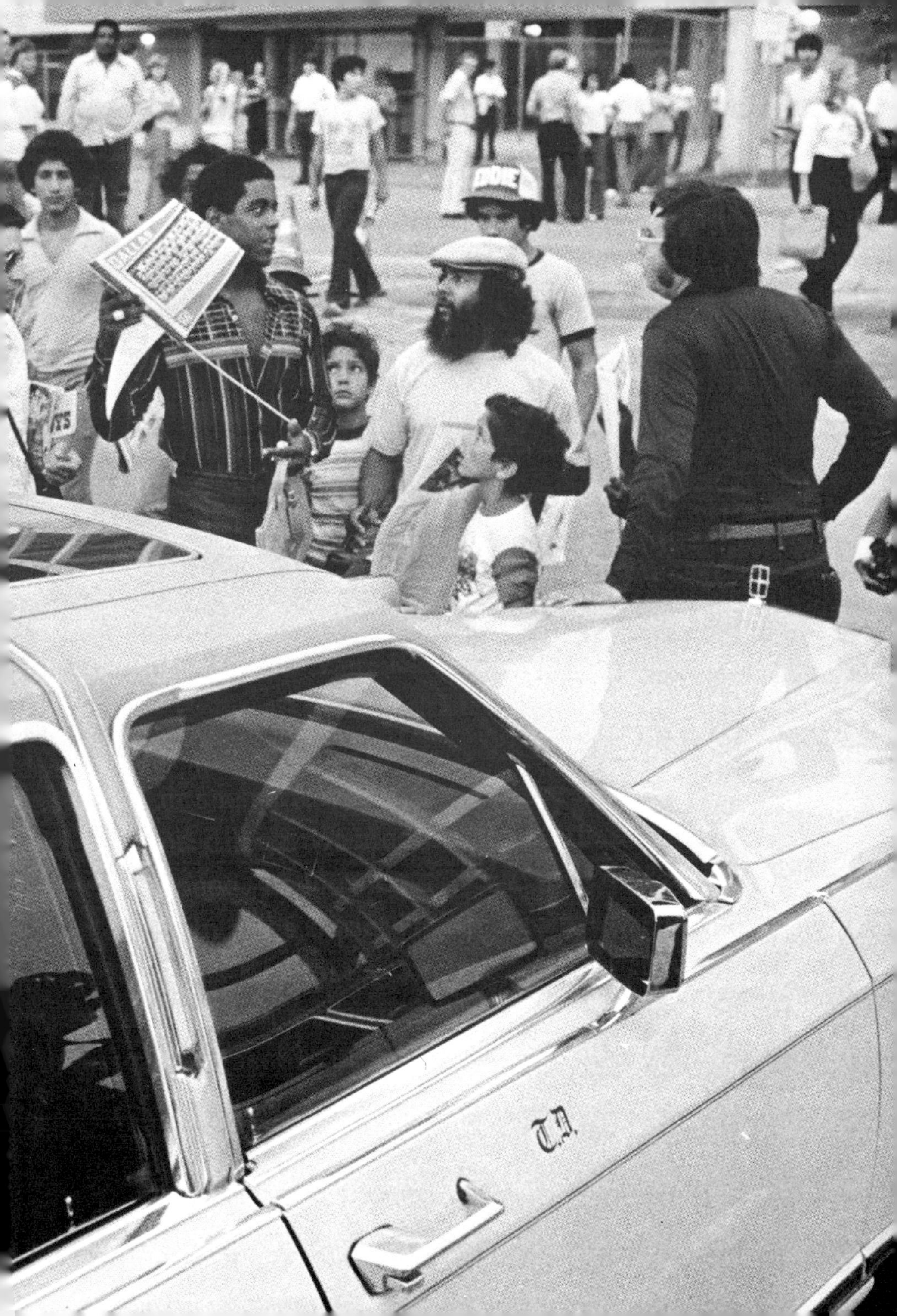
EDDIE
T.D.

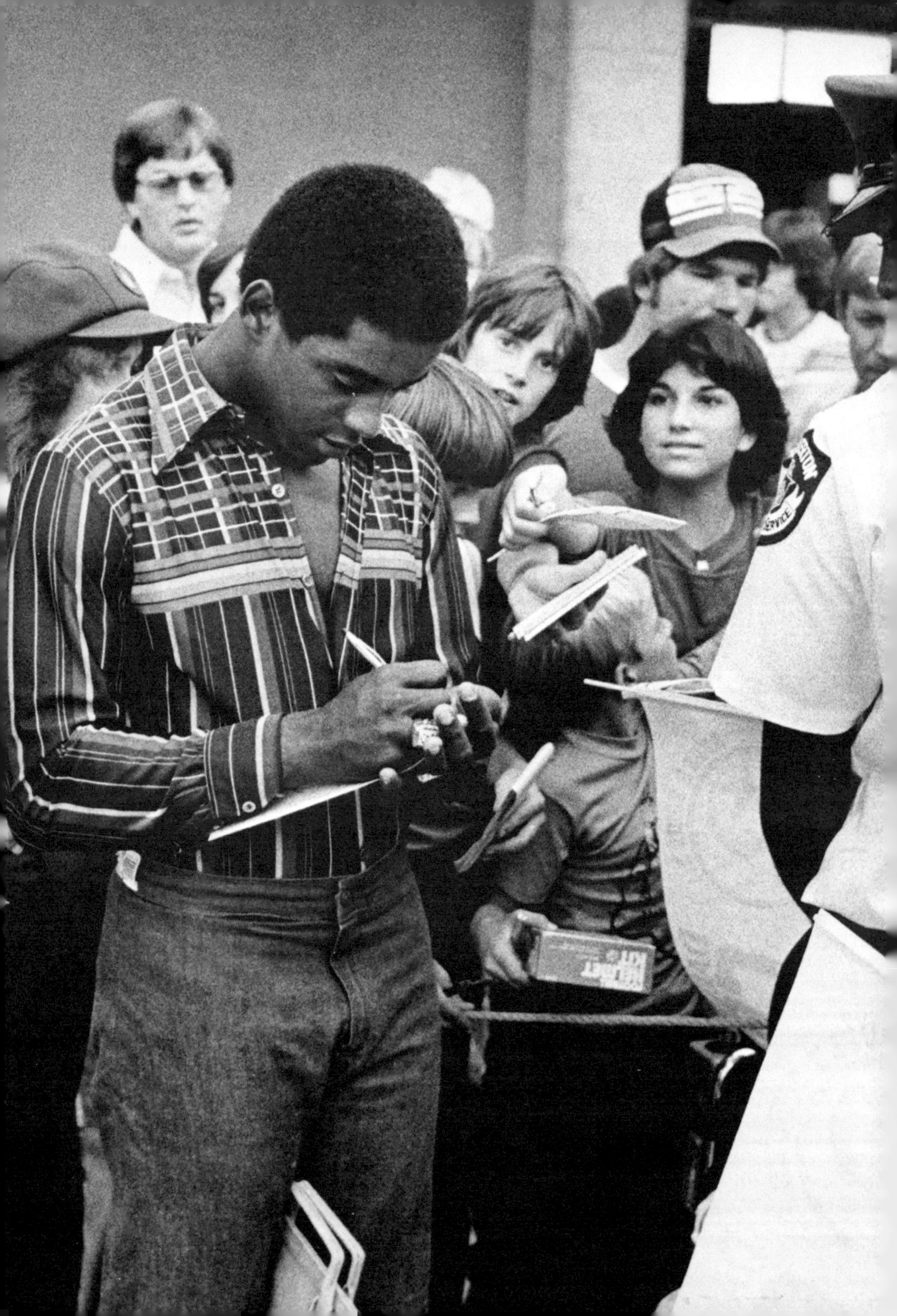

The Cowboys clinched their division title during a December game against Philadelphia. In that game Dorsett rushed for 206 yards. He scored two touchdowns. For one of them he made an 84-yard run.

The playoff games seemed almost too easy for the Dallas Cowboys. They rolled over the Chicago Bears and the Minnesota Vikings. They won the NFC title. They also won the right to go to the Super Bowl. They would play the Denver Broncos.

In the Super Bowl, Tony rushed for 66 yards. He scored the game's first touchdowns. But the big force in that game was the Dallas defense. It forced eight Bronco turnovers. The Cowboys beat Denver 27 to 10. Again, they made it look easy.

Tony Dorsett finished his first season. He rushed for 1,007 yards. His 84-yard run was the longest 1977 NFL run from scrimmage. He made 13 touchdowns. Second in the conference. Only Walter Payton scored more. Tony was named the NFL Rookie of the Year.

"Tony Dorsett is one tremendously gifted athlete," says O.J. Simpson. "When his career is over, there probably won't be many NFL records that won't have his name on them."

But Tony's career is not over yet. In the 1980-1981 season he rushed for 1,331 yards. He is the best running back in Cowboy history.

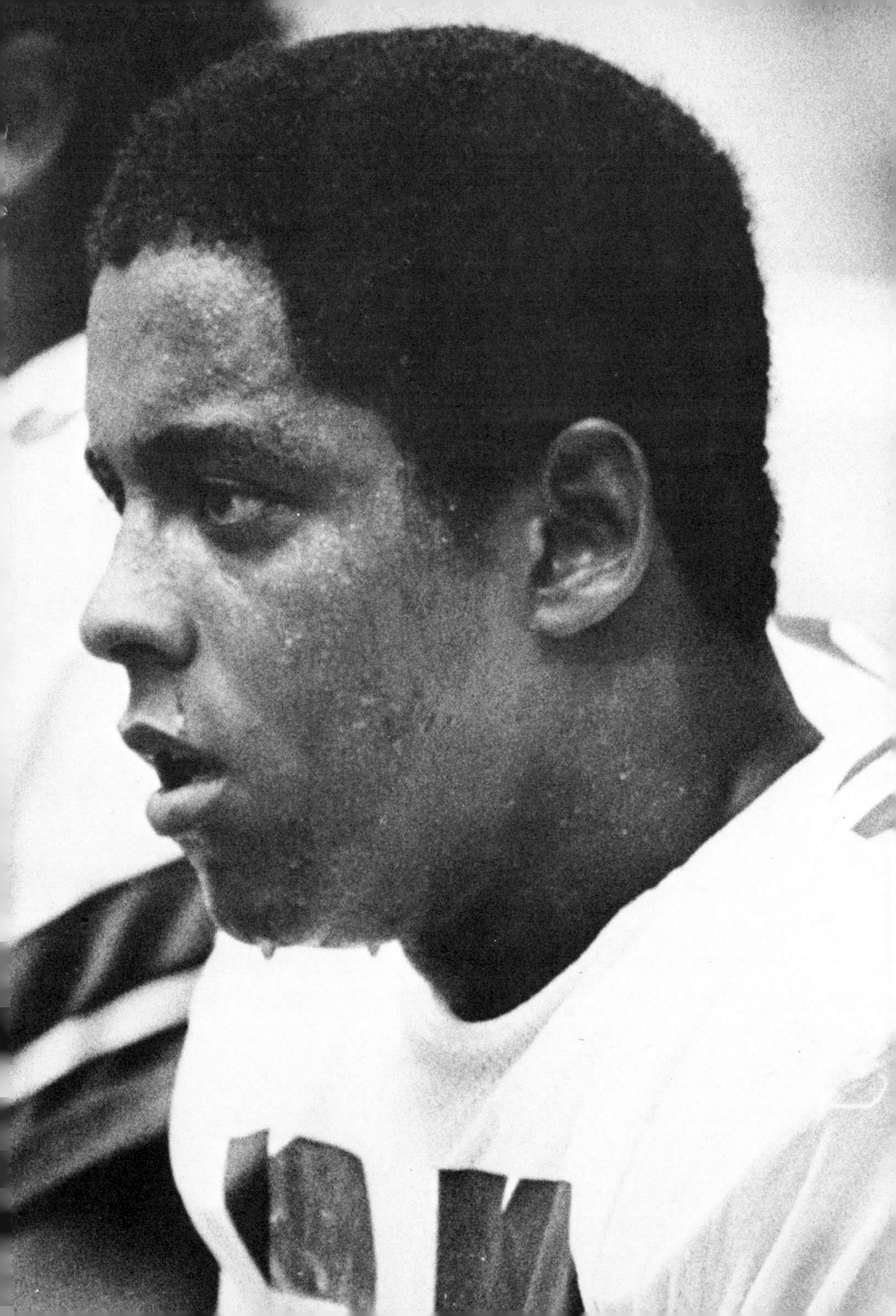

CHRONOLOGY

1954 — Tony was born on April 7.

1961 — At the age of seven Tony attempts to play football. His early efforts are failures because he is thin, small, and afraid of facing the bigger boys on the field.

1968 — Tony enters high school. He is still small, but even as a freshman he is faster than anyone else in school.

1971 — During his junior year in high school Tony is determined to become a great football player. He believes football is his only way out of the steel mill town where he was born.

1972 — Tony graduates from high school and enters the University of Pittsburgh where he becomes starting halfback. In his first year he runs for more than 1,500 yards, an amazing feat for a first year player running behind an inexperienced line.

1976
Nov. — In a game against Navy, Dorsett runs for 180 yards, giving him a total of 5,206 yards for his career. This sets a new record for yards gained by a college running back.

Dec. — Pitt smashes Penn State 24-7 in the last regular season game. Dorsett finishes with 6,082 yards gained during his college career, establishing a record that will probably last for many years.

Dec. — Tony Dorsett wins the Heisman Trophy as the best college football player of 1976.

1977
Jan. — On New Year's Day Tony sets a Sugar Bowl record by rushing for 202 yards. Pitt beats the Georgia Bulldogs 27-3 to become the national champions.

Aug. — Dorsett joins the Dallas Cowboys.

Sept. — The season opens with Tony sitting on the Dallas bench.

Dec. — Tony is now a starter, and in a game against Philadelphia he gains 206 yards to set a Cowboy record for yards gained in a single game. He also had one 84-yard touchdown run; this is the longest run from scrimmage in the NFL in 1977.

Dec. — The Cowboys easily beat the Chicago Bears and the Minnesota Vikings to advance to the Super Bowl.

1978 — Dallas overwhelms the Denver Broncos 27-10. Tony runs for 66 yards and scores the game's first touchdown.

1981 — Tony finishes the season with a record 1,331 yards rushing.

1980 — Tony rushed for 1,185 yards, an average of 4.3 yards per carry.
1981 — Tony finished his best season with 1,331 yards rushing, an average of 5 yards per carry.

ABOUT THE AUTHOR

In his youth Mr. Conrad was a mediocre basketball player, a poor baseball player, and an absolute disaster as a football player. Consequently, he spent many hours on the sidelines of athletic fields watching more gifted athletes perform. From an early age he became a fan.

Mr. Conrad has seen the great running backs in action. He was born in Chicago, and is a lifelong fan of the Chicago Bears. He has seen Gale Sayers, Jim Brown, O.J. Simpson, and other ball carriers. He thinks Tony Dorsett is one of the greatest.